The  7 Day

Bully-Buster

J. Alexander

First published in Great Britain in 2007 by Hodder Children's Books

This edition published by Hodder Children's Books in 2007

Text copyright © Jennifer Alexander 2007
Illustration copyright © David Whittle 2007
Design by Don Martin

The right of Jennifer Alexander and David Whittle to be identified as
the Author and Illustrator of this Work has been asserted by them
in accordance with the Copyright, Designs and Patents Act 1988.

3

A catalogue record for this book is available from the British Library.

ISBN-13: 978 0 340 93066 3

Printed in the UK by CPI Bookmarque, Croydon, CR0 4TD

The paper and board used in this paperback by Hodder Children's Books are
natural recyclable products made from wood grown in sustainable forests. The
manufacturing processes conform to the environmental regulations of the
country of origin.

Hodder Children's Books
A division of Hachette Children's Books
338 Euston Road, London NW1 3BH
An Hachette Livre UK Company

CONTENTS

Introduction   1

1 MONDAY
   Make the decision   16

2 TUESDAY
   Talk about it   35

3 WEDNESDAY
   Watch for the enemy within   48

4 THURSDAY
   Think positive   64

5 FRIDAY
   Face your fear   82

6 SATURDAY
   Stand up for your rights   94

7 SUNDAY
   Celebrate success!   109

Other titles in the Seven Day series:

The Seven Day Self-Esteem Super-Booster
The Seven Day Brain Booster
The Seven Day Stress Buster

INTRODUCTION

About bullying

Books about bullying always start with one of those bullet point lists of what bullying is – you know the sort of thing

- Name-calling

- Threats

- Ripping your arm off etc.

But this is no ordinary book about bullying, as you're about to find out, so let's just say:

If someone repeatedly tries to hurt or upset another person in any way at all, you can safely assume that it's bullying.

That's the definition – now let's talk about something more interesting ... you!

The all-about-you tick test

Tick any of the following that apply to you

1   I have been bullied

2   I am being bullied

3   I've seen other people being bullied

4   I'm scared of being bullied

5   I bully other people

6   I'm in a bullying group

7   I love reading interesting books

Results

If you ticked 1, 2 or 3: You're normal – at least 80% of kids in surveys say they've been picked on.

If you ticked 4: You're right – it can happen to absolutely anyone.

If you ticked 5 or 6: Well done on owning up – that's the first step to stopping.

If you ticked 7: Keep reading!

Actually, keep reading if you had any ticks at all, because I'm going to tell you three interesting things about bullying that not a lot of people know ...

Three things that not a lot of people know about bullying

1 Bullying is wrong, end of. It's simply never acceptable to blame it on the victim.

Bullies are very fond of trying to make you feel like it's your fault – they say 'You made me angry' or 'You shouldn't be so annoying.' Even your mum, who's just trying to help, might well start by asking 'What were you doing to annoy them?'

You are not responsible for someone else's
nastiness and aggression – they are. There is never
any excuse for attacking people, spreading nasty
rumours, making threats and all the other nasties
in the bullies' bag of tricks.

2 Teasing is serious too.

Everyone takes physical stuff seriously, but lots of
people think things like teasing, name-calling,
sending nasty texts and shutting someone out
aren't such a big deal. Well, excuse me! Non
physical bullying can be just as vicious and
damaging as punching and kicking.

Children have told ChildLine that they think
being teased can actually be more hurtful than
being pushed around. Bruises soon fade, but hurt
feelings can be harder to handle and take much
longer to heal.

3 You can learn not to let bullying hurt your feelings and make you feel bad about yourself.

This is good news twice over – for one thing, if
you get bullied it won't bother you so much, and
for another thing, if it doesn't bother you so
much, you're much less likely to get bullied again.

The art of bully-busting

The philosophy behind martial arts like Tae Kwon Do is that if everyone knew how to defend themselves the world would be a more peaceful place, because even really hard types might think twice about smacking someone who could drop-kick them half way to Korea.

But although knowing some Tae Kwon Do moves could be handy in a scrap, it might not be so useful if

- You're being got at by a gang (v. common because bullies aren't famous for their courage and sense of fair play).

- The bully is either armed or much bigger than you (also v. common – same reason).

- The bullying isn't physical – you can't really give people a slap for calling you names or just not talking to you.

What you need when it comes to physical bullying is to be able to recognise when you need help and have the courage and confidence to ask for it.

What you need when you're dealing with teasing and name-calling is to be able to let it go, like water off a duck's back.

This is bully-busting!

If everyone knew how to do it, there would be less bullying in the world, because it's simply no fun picking on someone who couldn't care less. There are seven main moves in bully-busting, designed to give victim feelings the boot.

Bully-busting – the seven main moves

1   Decide you can do something

Helplessness

2   Talk about it

Shame

3   Watch for the enemy within

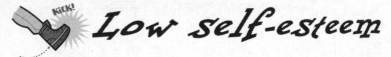

Low self-esteem

4   Think positive

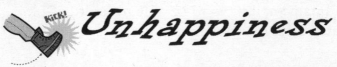

Unhappiness

5   Face your fear

6   Stand up for your rights

7   Celebrate success

By a happy coincidence, there are also seven days in a week, and that brings me to the beauty of this book.

About this book

There are seven chapters in this book – one for each day of the week – and each chapter covers one of the seven main bully-busting moves. All you have to do is read a chapter a day and pick something from the 'Choice of training sessions' at the end.

It's as easy as ABC:

A   Before you go to bed, read the chapter for the following day and decide which training session you're going to do.

B   When you get up in the morning, remind yourself what it is.

C   Some time during the day, do it!

Note: It's best to start on a Sunday evening, so if you're reading this on a Wednesday, sorry – you're just going to have to wait!

The 'seven day' system

'Wow!' I hear you say. 'This means I can get the hang of bully-busting in just one week!' Well, no … Bully-busting is like any self-defence martial art – it takes time to master. Understanding the theory isn't enough – you have to build up your fitness and keep practising the moves. So when you get to Sunday, you start all over again, choosing different training sessions.

By the end of the second week, you won't have to reread the chapters any more because they're very short and you'll be able to remember what's in them. You can just choose your training for each day and do it.

There are enough training sessions for a different one every day for ten weeks. If that sounds like a bit of a mission, worry not! The tasks are v. quick and simple, designed to help you build up fantastic bully-busting skills the way that ants build massive anthills one titchy grain at a time.

2 top training tips

1 Try to have a go at as many different training sessions as you can, but skip any that really don't appeal to you – enjoyment is the key to success.

2 Try not to miss a day. It's much better to do a really quick session you've done before than nothing at all.

One week will make a difference, two weeks will make twice the difference – the longer you keep it up the stronger you will feel.

Ten treats for ten weeks

If you decide to try for the full ten weeks, give yourself a little incentive. Every Sunday, buy a small treat and wrap it up like a present. Put it somewhere safe.

If you're doing the bully-buster with a mate, buy a little gift for each other or if you've got the sort of mum/dad/grandma/grandpa/ friend who likes helping, ask them to do it for you.

At the end of ten weeks of bully-busting it'll be like Christmas – you'll have ten lovely treats to unwrap and enjoy!

The seven-day system is brilliant because

● **It's easy**

The training sessions only take a few minutes each day but simply thinking about them reminds you to focus on bully-busting and not feel like a victim.

● **It's not scary**

None of the training sessions involve confronting bullies and bullying situations directly so you can practise your skills in less challenging areas of your life.

● **It works**

It's not about pretending you feel OK and in control – it's about really feeling OK and in control, so that you can recover your self-esteem if you have been bullied, not let it get to you if you are being bullied, stop feeling scared if you're afraid of being bullied and take action if you see it happening to someone else.

- ## It gives you skills for life

  When you know how to handle feelings of helplessness, shame and so on in relation to bullying, you can use those skills to overcome any problem life throws at you.

The seven-day bully-busting club

The seven-day approach is very flexible. You can do it by yourself if you like doing things on your own, but it's also great to share with other people.

You can do the training sessions with your best mate or a group of friends, and compare notes afterwards. You can do them with your mum or dad if you're in a family that likes doing things together. You can ask your teacher to start a seven-day bully-busting set at school.

It doesn't matter how you do it, as soon as you start you'll be part of the global seven day bully-busting club because everyone who's got this book, wherever they are in the world, will be choosing from the same ten training sessions on the same day as you. Imagine!

Ready, steady ... reminder time

Unless you happen to be reading this on a Sunday
evening, it's time to close the book now. Leave
yourself a reminder to start on Sunday somewhere
you can't miss it – on your mobile, say, or a note
beside the bed.

Ttfn! *

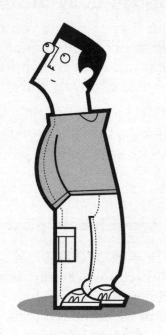

*Ta ta for now

INTRODUCTION

I said, close the book! Still, I knew you wouldn't, and actually there are a few things I'd like you to do before lift-off time on Sunday.

1 Get a special note pad

Some of the training sessions need a pen and paper (don't worry – they're all v. easy). You can scab bits of paper off your mum as you go along but if you do that you might lose them and then someone else might find them, which you might not want to happen as they will include some v. private things.

Your special note pad is like a diary – you might show it to some people but you wouldn't want the whole world and his dog to see it.

2 Find a secret hiding place

Not for you – for your note pad! Don't be slack and just shove it under your mattress – that's so unimaginative and besides, your mum would find it the minute she changed the sheets.

3   Make a record sheet

This is just for people who either like keeping record sheets or won't be able to remember which tasks they've done without one.

You could do it at the back of your special note pad if you've got one.

	Mon	Tues	Wed	Thurs	Fri	Sat	Sun
Week 1	5	2	10	4	2	7	6
2							
3							
4							
5							
6							
7							
8							
9							
10							

4   Think about getting some bully-buster buddies

If you decide someone you know might want to join in, get them on board now before you begin.

I think that just about does it, so now you really must close the book until Sunday evening, OK? I mean it!

1 MONDAY

Make the decision

Mental preparation – that's the first step on the road to anywhere and trying to start without it would be like setting off on a long drive with an empty tank.

In bully-busting there are two sorts of mental preparation:

- Accepting the challenge
- Getting information

Accepting the challenge

Bullying stinks, but it's a fact of life. As long as there are human beings in the world there will always be bullying, because aggressiveness and cruelty are part of human nature.

Some people don't like to accept that fact. Teachers may say things like, 'We haven't got any bullying in our school', bullies may say 'We were only having a laugh', and victims may believe them.

it happens!

Bully-busters have to start by facing facts and accepting that it happens.

Then they're ready to
move on to a second
astonishing and truly
life-changing fact ...

it makes great manure!

It's no good accepting that bullying happens and
then just throwing your hands up in dismay and
falling apart. You have to accept that it happens
and then decide what you're going to do about it.

When you do that, you might find that good
changes can grow out of the horrible experience
of bullying. Harry certainly did.

Harry's story

Harry and his family spent most weekends travelling round the country with a big group of people, dressing up in historical costumes and re-enacting battles from the English Civil War. It was fantastic fun, but not really the sort of thing Harry wanted his schoolmates to know about.

Sure enough, when they found out, they teased him about it all the time. If he got upset they said, 'We're just having a laugh.' So Harry felt doubly bad because he not only had a weird hobby, he couldn't take a joke either.

The teasing turned to pushing and shoving. One day, Harry's parents noticed he had bruises on his arms, and he told them he and his mates had just been larking around. His parents said you didn't usually get big bruises like that from having fun.

The penny dropped! Harry had to accept that his friends were really being horrible to him – not friendly at all in fact. Then he realised they were often like that – he'd actually joined in with them 'just having a laugh' about loads of other kids. But what could he do? Harry did the hardest thing he had ever done – he decided to get some new mates.

Harry's gang was the cool group at school, and they called the other boys sad losers, but when they saw him struggling, the losers were friendly. One of them, Jack, turned out to be a bit of a history nut. He persuaded Harry to let him tag along on a re-enactment weekend, and after that he was hooked!

Having Jack along made the weekends even better, and Harry was happier at school too, not having to worry any more about his secret coming out.

If Harry hadn't been bullied he would have stayed with his old friends out of habit, even though they weren't very nice and he had to keep his family hobby a secret from them. He faced up to the fact that he was being bullied and then he decided what to do about it.

You can always treat bullying as a challenge, like Harry did. I'm not saying that it's easy – but that's the point about challenges. They're supposed to be hard!

Bullying is a tough challenge. It can destroy you if you let it, but it can also teach you how to toughen up. Loads of famous people who were bullied at school say that learning to handle it was what gave them the determination and self-belief to become mega-successful. It also gave them the strength to cope with celebrity without crumbling, because everyone who's famous has to face the possibility of nasty rumours, ridicule and bad press.

Ten top celebs who found the going tough at school:

1 David Beckham

2 Charlotte Church

3 Sara Cox

4 Christina Aguilera

5 Tom Cruise

6 Sarah Michelle Gellar

7 Orlando Bloom

8 Janice Long

9 Kate Winslet

10 Eminem

When the going gets tough, the tough get going!

Getting information

Knowledge is power. You can do battle better if you know what back-up is available. Did you know, for example, that people who send abusive emails can be tracked by internet service providers and the police? Or that website hosts will close down bullying message boards? Or that, even if a caller conceals their number from you, they can still be traced? A lot of bullies and victims don't even realise that all forms of cyber bullying can be against the law because they amount to harassment.

When you know what help is available you can make an informed decision about whether to go for it. You can weigh up the risks and decide for yourself whether they're worth taking. Adults say you should always tell a teacher, but kids know that that won't always work and could be risky.

It's easy to find all the information you need in books and websites, but here's something you won't find anywhere else – my Risks and Benefits Guide to getting help.

The Risks and Benefits Guide

1   *Teasing, name calling and all non-physical kinds of bullying.*

Who could help teachers

Risks They might not believe you, they might think you're making a fuss, they could make it worse and other kids could call you a dobber.

Benefits On some occasions teachers can sort out non-physical bullying, especially if it's a misunderstanding. Sometimes people might really think teasing is 'just a laugh' and be quite shocked to find out how upset it makes you feel, and sometimes friends do fall out and stop talking just because they don't know a kinder way of getting a break from each other.

But it's much harder for teachers to deal with non-physical bullying because it isn't so clear what's going on or who's in the wrong.

2   *Physical bullying – punching and kicking, theft, damage to property etc.*

Who could help teachers, school governors, police

Risks Telling could make it worse, but it doesn't usually, and there's less chance people will think you're making a fuss. Also, the other kids wouldn't blame you so much for dobbing.

Benefits Schools are v. good at dealing with this because it's obvious who's in the wrong and witnesses aren't in any doubt about what they've seen.

Bullies aren't brave, so if it gets physical, chances are you're dealing with someone bigger than you or a gang. Reality-check time! You can't deal with this on your own.

Note: Start by telling a teacher rather than going straight to the governors or the police. Schools can almost always sort physical bullying out on their own.

Another note: You could cut your risks completely by reporting physical bullying you've seen or suffered anonymously via a bully box, naming the bullies and saying what they're doing.

Yet another note: If your school hasn't got a bully box, why not suggest that they get one? It's just like a post box for pupils to report bullying to the teachers and because you don't have to sign your letter nobody needs to know who sent it.

3   *Cyber bullying – Abusive txts, emails, phone-calls, message boards, blue-jacking and anything else they've dreamed up by the time this book goes to press*

Who could help police, internet service providers, phone companies

Risks of telling ISPs and phone companies Virtually nil – the bullies can be traced and stopped without you needing to be named, so tell your phone company or the ISP involved and forward nasty emails straight to whichever system the sender is using – the address is usually abuse@hotmail.com, abuse@btinternet.com, etc.

Risks of going to police Might feel scary, but still worth doing if the cyber stuff is particularly vicious or part of a serious bullying campaign.

Benefits If you stick to the golden rule and never respond in any way to abusive texts and emails, they usually stop on their own, because the sender isn't getting a reaction and they can't even be sure that you're receiving them. But if you do decide to tell, something can always be done because there's always evidence.

Bully-busting starts with making the decision to

- Accept that bullying happens and treat it as a challenge.

- Get the info you need about what help is available.

This is mental preparation and it carries absolutely no risk at all, but the benefits are huge because it means you don't have to feel helpless any more.

So get yourself down to the bully-busting gym and choose your Monday training session now!

Choice of Monday training sessions

❶ A message to your mind

We say things to ourselves all the time without even noticing.

And our minds believe them.

You can change your mind messages by choosing to talk to yourself in positive ways. This is called making affirmations, and loads of people find it very effective.

You don't have to believe that affirmations are true, they work anyway, but it can help to start with 'Right now' because in that single moment where nothing else exists you truly can be anything you like.

> Right now,
> I am
> letting it
> go.

If you are being bullied you can deal with feelings of helplessness by using affirmations like this.

Choose one of these and repeat it ten times before you get up. Then draw a dot on one of your fingernails as a reminder and repeat your affirmation to yourself every time you notice the dot throughout the day.

❷ The success rehearsal

Think of a time when you've been bullied or seen someone else being bullied and you didn't do anything about it. Write the story.

Take control by changing the ending so that things work out exactly the way you want them to. You can keep it realistic or give yourself special powers or get Godzilla in to help you – be as inventive as you like.

This lets you experience yourself in your imagination as a powerful person, and is a great rehearsal for success.

❸ Super celeb you!

If you were a celebrity, what kind would you be? A supermodel, football star, musician? Imagine yourself out there in front of the cameras – take your time – use all your senses to capture the scene – really enjoy it!

Remember way back when those losers at school were picking on you. Who's laughing now?

❹ 'I decided ...'

Think of a time you were bullied or saw someone else being bullied. Victim thinking goes like this – 'There was nothing I could do', 'They made me feel bad about myself' and 'They made me cry'.

Take control by seeing everything you did or didn't do as your own decision. Write this story by filling in the gaps:

What they did was (for example, call me a lamebrain) ... I decided to ... (for example, do nothing, feel bad about myself, cry) ... What I could have done was ... (for example, talk to Dad about it, tell Mrs Haddock, take no notice).

❺ Go to the experts

Check out these fantastic websites:

www.antibullying.net   www.bullying.co.uk

If you haven't got a home computer you can get access at the library or at school, or find a friend or relative who doesn't mind you using theirs.

Note: If you feel embarrassed looking up bullying sites, just say it's for a school project.

❻ Weighing up wisdom

Grant me the serenity to accept the things I can't change, the courage to change the things I can, and the wisdom to know the difference.

This is known as 'the serenity prayer' and it's exactly what you need when you're weighing up the risks and benefits of getting help with bullying. Copy it out, and really think about it.

Sometimes you can make bullying stop but sometimes you can't, especially if it's mostly meanness and name-calling. But you can always change the way you react to it, if you have the courage to try.

❼ Make manure

List five nasty things that have happened to you. For example, 'Lesley stopped talking to me', 'I got a tummy bug ...'

Now think of something good that came out of each one – 'I hung out with Harriet instead', 'Dad stayed home with me and taught me to play chess ...'

If you can't think of anything good that came out of them, write down something good that could have. Maybe you just sat and cried when Lesley wasn't talking to you – well, you could have hung out with Harriet instead.

⑧ Yah, boo, sucks to Cinders' sisters!

Cinderella is the classic bullying story. Read, write or draw a picture strip of the Cinders story. Here are the basic bits:

- Cinders gets pushed around by her two ugly sisters.

- They stop her going to the ball.

- Her fairy godmother magics up a nice frock and a coach for her to go in.

- Cinders wows the prince but she has to leave before the magic wears off at midnight.

- She drops her slipper.

- The prince goes looking for the girl who fits the slipper.

- Cue happy ending.

The happy ending comes in two parts – the mushy bit for Cinders and the prince, and the sisters' come-uppance. Make it as horrid as you like!

⑨ Ready, steady, record sheet

Make a record sheet for any incidents of bullying you suffer or witness – now you're ready to start recording!

Date and time	Place	Who was involved – descriptions if you don't know names	What they said or did to you	Names or descriptions of anyone who saw what happened

If you prefer, download a 'bullying sheet' from the ChildLine site **www.childline.org.uk** and check out the real-life stories while you're there.

⑩ Hah, so! Think martial arts

Martial arts involve mental focus and discipline as well as physical techniques. Find out if any classes are available near you. Get a book from the library.

Simply thinking about taking up a martial art is a way of feeling pro-active – but of course, if finding out makes you want to give it a try, I wouldn't want to stop you!

2 TUESDAY

Talk about it

Talking is not the same as telling. When you tell, you normally want the person to do something about it. When you talk, you're just getting things out in the open and off your chest.

Lots of schools now are trying to be 'talking schools', getting everyone to report any bullying they see and having discussions about the best ways of tackling the problem. If no one talks about bullying in a school or workplace, a family or friendship group, it can become like a guilty secret. Not talking is a way of protecting the bully.

Bullies are like vampires – they thrive in darkness. Let a bit of daylight in and expose them, and often they just crumble away.

Alice's story

Some older girls kept pinching the best things out of Alice's packed lunch. 'If you tell anyone, we'll get you after school,' they said. Alice kept quiet and pretended she didn't mind them taking her choccy bicks and strawberries.

But then they started making fun of her sandwiches too. She felt stupid and hated her stupid mum for making stupid cheese and pickle sandwiches that looked like poo.

Alice could hardly swallow a bite and she was always hungry, until one day she had had enough.

The big girls were late arriving for lunch and Alice told the other kids on her table what had been going on. It turned out they already knew because all of them had been picked on in exactly the same way. They asked the kids on other tables – half the school had had food pinched by the same big girls at one time or another.

The dinner ladies heard what they were all talking about. When the big girls arrived they had to sit on a table on their own. It was their turn to go hungry!

Considering that talking about bullying is such a good idea, why don't more people do it? Well, there are lots of things that can get in the way. Try the 'Listening ear' maze and see how tricky it is to get past all the obstacles.

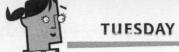

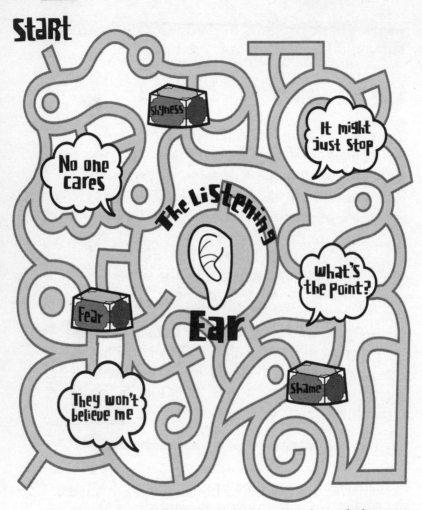

The biggest problem is getting started, and the secret is to choose who you talk to very carefully so that it feels safe. When it comes to who you choose, start with the A Team (Absolutely no worries!) and progress to the B Team (Be careful but could be good!) if you need to.

The A Team

You have absolutely no worries talking to someone who absolutely can't interfere. You could choose your dog, your diary, your pen friend in Canada, jo@samaritans, ChildLine or your favourite celebrity.

Just telling your story will make you feel much better and that might be enough. But if it isn't, the A Team is a great place to practise for the riskier business of talking to someone who might interfere. It will help you to organise your thoughts and feel calmer because often the first time you talk about painful things, you need some tissues handy!

The B Team

B Team people could be good because they have the power to help you if you want them to. Examples include – your parents or carers, your teacher or head teacher, your big bro or sis, your mates, fellow pupils involved in peer mentoring or buddy schemes.

Because B Team people also have the power to interfere, you need to decide beforehand whether you want them to do anything, and be sure to pick someone who won't just take over and ignore your wishes.

If you don't want them to do anything, say so. 'I'd just like to talk to you but I don't need any help right now.'

A problem shared ...

... is a problem halved, they say, and it's true. Some people – especially boys – think it's weak and wussy to talk about stuff that's troubling them, because they should be able to sort it out for themselves. But talking things over is a way of starting to sort them out, and it actually takes a lot of courage.

If you're not used to talking about your problems, you probably don't realise what a difference it can make, but as soon as you do you'll find that you

- feel better because shame grows on bad secrets like mould on an old sandwich.

- see things more clearly because you can't see something you're sitting on.

So give shame the boot ...

Kick! Shame

Go straight to the bully-buster gym and choose a 'talk about it' training session that's the right level for you today.

Choice of Tuesday training sessions

❶ A-B-let's see ...

Write down three people you know who could be on your A Team and three who could be on your B Team.

Next to each name, put the reason why they're on your list.

For example, 'ChildLine – Shona said they were really nice when she phoned them ...', 'Dad – he doesn't get into a flap about things like Mum ...', 'Miss Juniper – she handled that happy slapping last term really well.'

❷ Dear diary ...

Do a diary entry for your day. It doesn't matter if there's any bullying in it or not – simply expressing yourself and telling your own stories when nothing much happens makes it much easier to find your voice when you've got something difficult to say.

Note: If you enjoy this, you could start a diary now. Use a plain notebook so you aren't stuck with the same size section for every day and only write stuff when you feel like it.

❸ Have a chat

Have a conversation with an adult on any topic you like except bullying. You could talk to your teacher about the project you're doing, tell your

Dad what happened at the match or ask your mum how she got on at the office today, for example. You could phone your grandpa to talk about his hang-gliding holiday in Corsica ...

It's much easier to talk to an adult when something's bothering you if chatting to adults is part of your normal everyday life.

❹ Write a letter ... and destroy it!

This is a great way of getting things out of your system. Think of a bullying situation and write a letter to anyone you feel angry with about it. This could be someone who was picking on you or your mate, an adult who made it worse, or a witness who didn't speak up, for example.

You can make it as angry and outrageous as you like because you're not going to send it. No, really – even if it's completely brilliant, which it probably will be as it's fuelled by fury, you absolutely can't send it, OK?

Then tear the letter up into tiny pieces and throw them in the bin or bury them. Good riddance!

⑤ Write a letter ... and send it!

Tell your bullying story to a magazine problem page or bullying website or post it in your school's bully box. You don't have to put your real name. If you haven't got any bullying problems at the moment, write your opinions and suggestions instead.

If you've decided to talk to someone on your B Team, write a letter to them first. It's easier to remember everything you want to say in a letter. It's also easier to start a conversation with someone who already knows.

❻ The inside-outside pic

Get a sheet of paper, a glue stick, some scissors and a couple of old magazines. Tear bits out – words, patterns, images, colours – that feel like the face you show to the world. Do you seem calm like blue, happy like yellow, angry like red? Do you chat and smile a lot, or sit quietly at the back? Do you seem more like a holiday beach or a church? Stick your scraps on the paper, covering the whole surface.

Now flip the paper over and do the whole thing again, this time tearing stuff out that shows what's going on inside, the secret you, the things you like to hide. Are you secretly gloomy and dark, or calm like a summer meadow? Do you want to run away like a frightened rabbit, or blow your top like a volcano? Stick your scraps on, until the whole piece of paper is covered.

Are the two sides similar or completely different? What does that say about you?

❼ The facts and feelings fill-in

Think about three bullying situations you've seen or been involved in. Write down the facts and how you feel by filling in the gaps.

... I feel ... and what I want is ...'

ar example, 'When Jason pulls my hair I feel annoyed and I want to throttle him till his eyes pop', 'When Sandy calls me fat I feel embarrassed and I want the floor to swallow me up', 'When people pick on that little kid with the limp I feel guilty for not stopping them and I want to tell someone.'

❽ Picture this

Do a picture strip of something that happened in the day – it doesn't have to be about bullying. Maybe you couldn't find any clean socks or your teacher got cross with you about something you didn't do. Stick men and speech bubbles will do fine if you're not keen on drawing.

Telling the small simple stories of things that happen in your life is great practice for when you've got a more difficult story to tell, like when you're being bullied.

❾ Songs that speak for you

Write down the first five fave songs that come into your head. If you can, listen to them. Feel the emotions in them, think about the words.

Jot down a few notes beside each one – 'sad, she feels betrayed ... happy, silly, party, dance ...'

Your favourite songs express the feelings that are strong in your life right now.

⑩ The bigger picture

People are most vulnerable to bullying when they've got other stressful things going on in their life, like starting a new school, parents arguing a lot or an illness in the family.

Notice if there's anything bothering you at the moment. Choose an A Team person to talk to about it.

3 WEDNESDAY

Watch for the enemy within

If you get picked on your self-esteem can take a battering. This can happen to anyone, so if you've never been picked on and you feel pretty good about yourself, still read this chapter. Very few people can stand up to bullying that goes on for a long time or kicks in when they're feeling particularly vulnerable, for example during a family break-up.

Tiresome but true – 1

Bullying can get anybody down. And it's a slippery slope ...

As soon as your confidence is dented, bullies will make a beeline for you, so low self-esteem isn't just an effect of bullying, it's also a cause.

Tiresome but true – 2

Bullies love to kick a person when they're down.

Considering how important it is, a lot of people don't really understand what self-esteem is all about. Do the self-esteem checklist and see if you're in the know.

The self-esteem checklist

Here are ten statements about self-esteem. Tick any that you think are true.

To have high self-esteem you need to

1   Be good-looking

2   Have loads of friends

3   Be sporty

4   Wear cool clothes

5   Have plenty of money

6   Be good at schoolwork

7   Like being yourself

8   Be fit and healthy

9   Live in a normal family

10 Think you're better than everyone else

Answers

Only one of the statements is true. If you had more than one tick, go back through them now and see if you can tell which one it is.

The only thing you need in order to have high self-esteem is to like being yourself. That's what self-esteem is – liking, respecting and accepting yourself just as you are. You can be poor and have high self-esteem, you can be plain. You can be a loner or have a disability. Anyone can have high self-esteem because it doesn't depend on what you've got or how you look – it's purely a question of how you feel about yourself.

Bullies want you to feel bad about yourself, because that makes you weak – you can't stick up for somebody you don't like. They've got two main ways of undermining you by

- making you believe a bad thing about yourself that isn't true,

  or

- making you believe that a true thing about yourself is bad.

51

If it isn't true, don't go there!

It can be easier to take no notice of insults that obviously aren't true but if they go on long enough or come from someone you think of as a friend, you can start to wonder.

Supposing people call you ugly when you aren't – that's surprisingly common and it happens to lots of top models all the way through school. It shouldn't bother you because it's ridiculous. But if it does start to get to you, you might think 'Actually, maybe I am a bit fat, maybe my chin is too big …'

Supposing Big Dan and his mates are pushing you around and they taunt you for being feeble – that's stupid because even Big Dan couldn't stand up to a gang of six. But if it starts to get to you, you might think, 'They're right – I am puny and pathetic.'

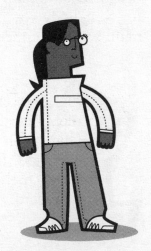

If you start thinking that bad things people say about you might be true, you're actually taking their side against yourself. That's what Hannah did.

Hannah's story

Hannah had a cute little dog called Minnie who always followed her around. When Hannah got a skateboard for Christmas, Minnie had to have a go too, and by the end of the holiday, she was as good as Hannah!

Hannah told her friends about Minnie's skateboarding skills when term started again – she felt so proud. But her so-called friend Gems said it was cruel to make dogs do tricks and they could report Hannah to the RSPCA. Hannah was shocked and confused.

She didn't think that she had been cruel. She certainly hadn't meant to be cruel. But if Gems said she was ... Hannah felt ashamed of herself and stupid too, for not even realising that it was cruel to let Minnie go on the skateboard.

The other kids joined in criticising Hannah and she couldn't argue because she thought she deserved it. Which of course made everyone, including Hannah, even more sure that they were right!

If it is true, is it really so bad?

Often, like in Hannah's story, people say things out of jealousy or spite that just aren't true. But what if they are? Then you're bound to believe what they say, and doesn't that mean you've got to be on their side?

Maybe you wear glasses and they call you 'speccy four eyes' or you've got red hair and they call you 'ginger nut'. Maybe you get teased for being overweight or underweight or tall or short or having sticky-out ears. Maybe you get teased for wearing hand-me-down clothes or the wrong trainers. Bullies often target the way you look.

Well, it still doesn't have to bother you. You can agree with them that you've got ginger hair or whatever, but you don't have to beat yourself up about it. Be nice to yourself. There's nothing wrong with having ginger hair – or being tall or short etc. – so why should you feel bad?

People of all shapes and sizes find friends and partners who totally love them just as they are – in fact, being mean and spiteful is much more of a handicap when it comes to finding love.

But even if mean people find something you just couldn't like about yourself in a million years, it's still not the end of the world.

If it really is so bad – so what?

Liking yourself doesn't mean you have to like every little thing about yourself any more than liking your best mate means you have to like every little thing about them. Maybe their hair's a bit frizzy or their teeth stick out or they don't get the hang of new video games very quickly. Sometimes they might do annoying things or wear clothes that look stupid or make a fool of themselves.

With a friend, you enjoy the things you like about them and accept the rest.

If someone teases you for your faults and foibles just remember that nobody's perfect, even you. Shrug and say 'Fair enough!' then let it go. Be a good friend to yourself and focus on the things you like about being you.

Low self-esteem is the enemy within, so give it the boot!

Start right now by choosing a lovely Wednesday workout.

Choice of Wednesday training sessions

❶ You've got a friend

Buy or make a special gift for yourself as a token of friendship. Make it something you can wear or carry around in your pocket, so it's a constant reminder of your promise to be a great friend to yourself.

It doesn't have to be anything fancy or expensive – a string wristband or a special pebble will do – its power is in its symbolic meaning.

❷ The friendship letters

Write a letter to yourself about a bullying situation that's bothering you. Start it 'Dear ... (your name)' and take your time. Put in all the details and your feelings about it. Really spill!

Now read the letter as though it had come from a close friend. How does it make you feel? What do you want to say to them?

Write a reply.

This second letter will contain all the support and advice you need to give yourself when you're dealing with bullying.

Note: You can use the two-letters technique for any problem, not just bullying.

❸ Check the checklist

Go to the self-esteem checklist on page 50 and make a list of opposites, for example:

1 Not good looking

2 Not many friends

3 Not sporty

... and so on.

Leave out number 7.

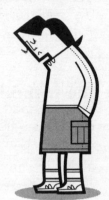

Now think of celebs or people you know who seem happy with themselves even though they aren't good-looking, etc.

1 Not good-looking – Homer Simpson (OK, he's not real either, but he's pretty convincing!)

2 Not many friends – my cousin Jake

3 Not sporty – our head teacher

... and so on.

❹ Radiators and drains

Notice the way that different people around you make you feel. Some people are radiators – they give out positive vibes and make you feel warm and happy. Other people are drains – they sap your energy and make you feel tired and fed up.

Think about how you can spend more time with radiators and less time with drains. This doesn't mean avoiding mates who may be having a hard time at the moment, but avoiding people who are always grumbling or having a go at you and never make you feel good.

❺ Help someone

This is a top self-esteem booster. Volunteer to help with the school jumble sale or any local fund-raiser. Offer to walk your sick neighbour's dog or tidy your gran's garden or do the washing-up.

Even something very tiny will give you the feel-good factor that comes from having other people really appreciate you.

❻ Chalk and cheese

Comparing yourself with other people is bad for your self-esteem plus it's v. silly because people are much more than the things you single out to compare.

Chalk isn't as tasty as cheese (I'm guessing) but that's only part of the picture. When it comes to making marks on a blackboard, give me chalk any time.

Make a list of three people you feel jealous of and why. For example, 'I'm jealous of Fiona Priest because all the boys like her'.

Now think of something they might feel jealous of you for. 'Her mum and dad have split up and my family's still together ...'

❼ Play your cards right

Everyone's born with a different set of strengths and limitations. Astrologers say it's in your stars at birth, and scientists say it's in your genes. Some people are just naturally more beautiful or talented, creative, practical or plain. The trick is to do the best you can with what you've been given.

Any card game will give you the experience of trying your best with the hand you've been dealt, sometimes winning and sometimes losing, just as in life you may win hands down in the looks department but lose out on A grades in school. You don't have to win every hand to enjoy the game!

If you don't know how to play cards, ask around. Find someone to play with and give it a go.

⑧ People watching

You can do people watching any time you're out and about, say on the way to school or sitting in the park or walking round the shops. Look out for people in pairs and groups. Notice how anyone can find friends and be loved whatever they're like – fat, thin, old, young, spotty, shabby, loud, shy … Even people who've got completely sad trainers can still be someone's perfect mate.

⑨ The reality check

In a perfect world we'd all be perfect, but in the real world we aren't. Wanting to be perfect means you're doomed to fail and that makes it the kiss of death to your self-esteem.

Real life is made up of good-and-bad, and although it's good to try always to be the best you can you also have to accept that you're never going to be perfect.

Write down five things you don't like about yourself, for example 'I've got greasy hair' or 'I'm rubbish at singing.' Then add a 'but' to each one – 'I've got greasy hair but a really nice smile' and 'I'm rubbish at singing but I'm great at painting.'

⑩ A secret reminder

Bullying can make you think, 'I hate being me' and then your mind will start gathering evidence for that idea, pulling together all the things you don't like about yourself, like a prosecution lawyer making a case.

If you tell yourself, 'I like being me' you'll gradually become more aware of all the things you like about yourself.

Write a secret reminder to yourself – ILBM – in five places you're bound to see it during the day. Every time you see it, say it, and get your mind working for the defence.

4 THURSDAY

Think positive

Being bullied makes you feel miserable and being miserable makes you feel weak. That's why an important part of bully-busting is knowing how to hold on to your happiness.

No one can be happy when they're actually being taunted or pushed around but no one's ever being taunted and pushed around 24:7. The trick is to separate the bad stuff from the good and not let your feelings about the bullying take over your whole life like Dom did.

Dom's story

Dom was being teased by another boy in his class because he was very tall. The boy called him 'Lofty' and said things like 'What's the weather like up there?' For ages, it didn't bother Dom at all, but when everyone started joining in it really got to him.

After that, Dom's average day would go like this.

8am – Dom wakes up in a bad mood because he's being teased.

(Is he being teased at this very moment? No!)

8.10 – Dom's dad tells everyone a new joke he's heard (What's on the sea-bed covered in chocolate? An oyster egg – ba-boom!) Dom isn't laughing because he's being teased.

(Is he being teased at this very moment? No!)

8.30 – Dom's mates call for him because it's fun walking to school together. Dom isn't finding it fun because he's being teased.

(Is he being teased at this very moment? No!)

You get the picture. Dom's whole day can turn out miserable just because at some stage he thinks someone might say something mean.

Let's look at the maths.

There are 24 hours in a day – that's 1440 minutes. A taunt, shove or other bullying incident lasts on average maybe 30 seconds. Say you experienced 10 bullying incidents in a day that would be a total of 5 minutes. 5 minutes out of 1440 – that makes ... hmm, let me see ... a very small percentage indeed! A tiny fraction! (Sorry – sums aren't really my strong point.)

You might not be able to feel cheerful when someone's actually having a go at you, but all the rest of the time you can, and that's the area you have to concentrate on. Building up happy feelings in the rest of your life means that if you do get picked on you'll be harder to knock down and quicker at bouncing back.

So here's a simple two-part strategy for holding on to your happiness whatever happens –

1   Bump up the good stuff.

2   Make the best of the bad.

Bumping up the good stuff

First ...

... you have to notice it.

Don't be like Dom and get so fixated on the bad stuff that you forget what a great dad you've got and how much you like your mates.

Next …

… enjoy it!

Be grateful. Gratitude is always a top tonic when it comes to happiness.

Finally …

… when it comes to the good stuff get as much as you can!

Think about the things you do and see if you could choose more happy activities. Do you watch TV programmes about mass murderers and horrible illnesses? Do you watch the News? Thinking about it now, would you say those programmes make you feel more cheerful? Change the channel!

Do you get plenty of fresh air and exercise? For maximum happiness, you need at least 20 minutes a day outside in natural daylight and a spot of physical exertion. Exercise makes your brain produce as much serotonin (happy chemicals) as a tablet from the doctor.

Do you spend time with other people? Nothing

makes you happier than feeling appreciated and loved. You don't need to have loads of friends or an absolute best mate because anyone will do – a parent, a pen pal, a pet.

Making the best of the bad

Bad things happen to everyone – fact. And here's another fact – everyone reacts to them differently. Do the quiz and find out how you normally respond to the bad things in life.

The six setbacks quiz

1 It's dinner-time and there's no pizza left. Do you think

   A It's no big deal – I'll just have chips.

   B I'm not having anything then!

   C This is my chance to try the new veggie rolls instead.

2 **You fell over the dog and now you've got a broken arm. Do you think**

A   It's just a broken arm.

B   Now I won't be able to do anything and I'm going to fall behind.

C   If this hadn't happened, I'd never have learnt how to write with my left hand.

3 **Your whole class is being kept in just because one or two kids were larking around. Do you think**

A   It's only one break time.

B   I don't want to be in this class any more.

C   I can use the time to catch up with my homework.

4 **It's the biggest match of the season and you haven't been picked for the team. Do you think**

A   There's always next time.

B   I'm not going to training any more.

C   This is my chance to go along and support my mates like they do when I'm the one on the field.

5 **Your mum's had a go at you because your bedroom's such a tip. Do you think**

A   It's a fair cop.

B   She's always getting at me.

C   If I tidy it up I might find those joke books I was looking for.

6 Your best mate seems more interested in getting to know the new kid than hanging out with you. Do you think

A It's just a fad.

B Another great friendship bites the dust.

C Since my mate's keen, I could get to know the new kid too.

Answers. If you got mostly

A – You take the rough with the smooth – that makes you hard to rattle.

B – You let things wind you up – that makes you every bully's favourite person.

C – You grab your problems by the throat and make them work for you – hah – so!

The strongest way of responding to the bad stuff is by asking 'What can I learn?' All

problems take you outside your comfort zone –
that's why they're a problem. You have to find
new strengths in yourself if you want to deal with
them – that's why they're a learning opportunity.

Bullying is a massive learning opportunity, but it
might be asking a lot of yourself to try and see
that straight away. The easiest way to get there is
in small steps by practising looking for the
learning in minor setbacks in the rest of your life,
and feeling how it works.

Give blues the boot!

Being happy is a positive personal choice. It's a
tough choice sometimes and you may have to
work at it, but if you can manage it even when
other people are trying their hardest to make you
miserable, that'll give you a fantastic feeling of
power.

Bully-busters be aware ...

1 Revenge is sweet.

2 Happiness is the best revenge!

So bump up the good stuff and make the best of the bad because that's the secret of holding on to happiness whatever life might throw at you.
Big smile!

Choice of Thursday training sessions

❶ Mind your language!

For a whole day, try to avoid negative words like 'can't', 'impossible', 'difficult', 'hopeless' and 'never'.

Get your friends or family to join in if you like, for all of dinner-time or an hour in the evening – unless that's too difficult, of course!

❷ Say thank you

Think of five things you love about your life. Count them off on your fingers. Now say thank you – it's as easy as that!

Do it first thing in the morning and last thing at night. Feels great, doesn't it?

Note: If you make this a habit and do it every day, choosing different things, it will change your life. Honest! If you don't believe me, try it and see.

❸ Film fun

Get a video or DVD of a comedy film and have a good laugh. Laughing is incredibly good for you. Even if you don't find the film very funny, laugh anyway – your brain pumps out happy chemicals every time you laugh or smile – it doesn't make any difference if you're just putting it on.

❹ The power of distraction

Set your alarm clock/mobile/stop watch to go off in fifteen minutes. Then get stuck into a book/ magazine/computer game/jigsaw puzzle.

When the alarm goes off, stop what you're doing. Notice what's going on in your head. While your brain's busy doing other stuff, it can't stay stuck in unhappy thoughts.

Note: If it's a good book/mag/game/jigsaw, do carry on. I wouldn't want to stop you enjoying yourself!

❺ Plan your happy TV week

Get a TV guide for the coming week. Go through it putting a ring round all the funny programmes and dramas you'd like to see, avoiding anything gloomy, worrying or violent.

For the rest of the week, only watch the programmes you've put a ring around.

Note: If you normally watch TV with your family, see if you can get your parents to join in. Tell them it's part of your bully-busting training if you think that might persuade them.

❻ The stop dot

Draw a dot on your thumbnail as a reminder and every time you notice it – stop.

Check out what you can see around you and home in on one thing like a cameraman zooming in for a close-up. A pen, a blade of grass, a crisp packet, a mobile phone, a pigeon ...

Really examine it for a few seconds – its colours and shapes – and think about how incredibly amazing it is. Every single thing is a miracle, but we're so busy we hardly ever notice it.

❼ Favourite things pic

Draw or get a photo of yourself and stick it in the middle of a piece of paper.

Surround yourself with all your favourite things – draw them, tear pics out of magazines, use photos, just write the words or do a glorious mixture of all four.

Four – that's my favourite number! Then there's the colour red, dragonflies, peanut butter, anything stripy, my rabbit ...

Put your picture on your bedroom wall where it can give you a happy boost whenever you need it.

❽ Make music

Make a CD or tape of songs that make you smile. These might include upbeat pop songs with cheery lyrics, old singalongs from holiday car journeys, that Status Quo thing your dad plays air guitar to, music from films you've enjoyed and anything else you can think of. Try to get at least five.

❾ Your two days

Write the story of all the bad things that happened during the day. 'I woke up late so all I had for breakfast was a measly custard cream in the car ...' Have a good grumble!

Now write the story of all the good things that happened. 'Mum gave me a lift because I was running late. Jez gave me that book he's always going on about ...'

See how having a good day or a bad day is a question of what you focus on.

10 Get moving

Write a list of five things you could do to get your body moving and give your brain a happy boost – for example, walk the dog, get out the dance mat, have a kick-around, run up and down the stairs ten times, go swimming.

Do one!

5 FRIDAY

Face your fear

Here's a silly joke with a serious point –

What do you get if you cross a crocodile with a rose?

I don't know, but I'm not going to smell it!

The point is that fear has a purpose – to keep you safe. Two purposes actually, because it also helps you to prepare for tackling danger. Although it feels like a weakness, it's actually part of your power to defend yourself, and that's why bully-busters need to know how to harness it.

Rule one – don't run!

Not, don't run away from scary things –
sometimes that's only sensible, like if your big sis
is on the warpath because you borrowed her iPod
without asking. But don't run away from fear.

Fear feels horrible, so most people avoid it as
much as they can. They

● dodge and deny it, as in 'I'm not scared, I just
don't fancy taking a short-cut down smokers'
alley.'

● try to get it over with quickly by being
reckless, as in 'I'll take the short cut and worry
about it later.'

● hide, as in 'I'm not going anywhere! I want to
just stay indoors and watch TV for the rest of
my life.'

Running away from fear means two things –

1 Your life gets smaller because you can't take
risks and trying new things always involves
risk.

2 Your fear gets bigger because it's got you beat.

If you have the courage to stop and look you almost always find that the actual danger is much smaller than your monster fear.

What's the worst that can happen if someone teases you? You might feel embarrassed or upset. Could you survive that? Of course you could! In fact, learning to survive embarrassment is linked to success in life – the most successful people are the ones who can fall flat on their face and still stand up again even though everyone's laughing.

But supposing it's worse than just teasing, maybe they push you or take your stuff. What's the worst that could happen then? Maybe some bruises and losing your mobile phone. Would your life be at risk? I don't think so. When fear is out of proportion, looking at it square on can help you to cut it down to size.

But if you are in real physical danger, facing up to your fear means it can show you what you need to do in order to stay safe.

Rule two – Do what you need to do

Supposing you've been threatened by someone who actually has beaten up other kids ... and say he hangs out in smokers' alley? Taking that short cut would be mad! Be scared and be safe – don't go there.

If you met him on your own, you could be in trouble, so what could you do about that? Be scared and be safe – make sure you're with a group of mates as much as possible.

What else could you do? Tell an adult. You might not want to, but being scared and knowing you're right to be scared will give you the push you need to do it.

Cara got scared for her friend, Lou, and that drove her to take action.

Cara's story

One day, Cara heard some girls in her class planning to ambush Lou on the way home from school. They were going to smack her around while one of them took photos on her mobile.

Cara felt really scared for her friend. She could have dodged and denied her fear by saying 'I'm not scared, it's none of my business.' She could have tried to get rid of it quickly by recklessly tackling the gang right there and then about what they were planning to do. She could have run away from it by going straight home and skipping school for the next few weeks till everything blew over.

But Cara faced up to her fear. She assessed the real risk and decided she had to do something about it. She warned Lou to take a different route home that afternoon, and the two of them decided to talk to their head teacher in the morning.

Facing it and doing what you have to do is how to deal with specific fears, but if bullying goes on for a long while you can get into a general state of nervousness and anxiety.

The fear that comes from bullying can infect the rest of your life like an illness, just the same way that the unhappiness from being bullied can do. Then you feel on edge all the time and everything seems scary. What if you get bitten by a rabid bat? What if you forget your bus fare? What if someone kidnaps your cat?

Cutting your anxiety levels generally will make it much easier for you to cope with your specific fears about bullying.

The anxiety attack

Attack your anxieties on two fronts by

● always expecting the best, and

● trusting you'll handle it, whatever happens.

Expecting the worst could be a definition of anxiety – it isn't about the present moment but what might happen in the future. No one knows what will happen in the future, so it makes no more sense to expect the worst than to expect the best. You can choose.

The benefits of expecting the worst are that you won't get any nasty surprises or disappointments in the future. The drawback is – it completely wrecks your life right now!

The benefits of expecting the best are that you live in a state of happy anticipation, and that makes you feel confident and strong. But what if ...

If the disaster happens, you'll handle it. This is a simple fact of life. People in war zones and epidemics and situations of extreme hardship just get on with it. Check it out in your own life. Think about the hardest things that have ever happened to you. You're still here, so guess what? – you handled it!

The experience of courage

Fear feels bad. But dodging it doesn't feel any better. In fact, it means the fear gets bigger until it overshadows your whole life and has you on the run. If you can bear the bad feeling of fear long enough to find out what it's telling you and take action – that feels good! It's the experience of courage, and you can't get it any other way.

You're bound to feel scared in a bullying situation – you can't avoid it. So face it, feel it, find out what it wants you to do. That's the only way to give your fear the boot.

Are you nervous about your Friday training? Come back! You know what you have to do ...

Choice of Friday training sessions

❶ Excuses, excuses

Write down five things you avoid doing and the reasons why, for example:

● Taking the bus into town instead of cadging a lift off dad.

Reason – It's easier and Dad doesn't mind.

- Saying hello to the new kid next door.

  Reason – He might turn out to be a pain.

- Joining the school volleyball club.

  Reason – I haven't tried and I probably won't be any good.

Think about each one carefully. Could you really be avoiding them out of fear? Are your reasons really excuses?

❷ One little fear

Fear is like a boundary around your life – rational fears keep you safe but the little irrational ones make your life much smaller than it needs to be. The more you manage to push through your small fears, the bigger your life becomes.

Do something today that you're a little bit scared of doing. It's supposed to feel scary, so don't bottle it!

Note: Only do this with small irrational fears – don't do it with big, sensible fears like skating on thin ice or patting next door's pit bull.

❸ Five BIG fears

Think of five BIG fears. Be specific, so not just 'I might die' but 'I might scratch myself and get flesh-eating disease' or 'There might be a war and our house could get blown up.'

Rate them on a scale of one to ten on how likely you think they are to happen.

If the risk of your big fears happening is less than five out of ten, it makes more sense to assume they won't happen than worry that they might.

❹ Fearless you

List five people, characters or animals that you think of as completely fearless – Superman, lions, my Uncle Jim, boa constrictors, Marge Simpson ...

Get a picture of one of them from a magazine or off the internet, or draw one.

Find a photo of yourself, cut out the face and stick it on your fearless person picture. Say hello to fearless you!

⑤ Go on an adventure

Read any adventure story – they always involve real physical danger. Be right there with the hero, facing fear, finding courage ... feeling fantastic!

⑥ I'll survive!

Whenever you have a setback throughout the day think, 'I'll survive!'

You forget your swimming stuff? Say 'I'll survive.' You're too late for pizza at lunchtime ... Big Ryan calls you a wuss ... You only get six out of ten in your test? Get things into perspective and say 'I'll survive.'

⑦ Picture this

Lie down on your bed and take three slow breaths so that you feel nice and relaxed. Close your eyes. Imagine yourself going way, way back in time, across the centuries, to a prehistoric land.

Take your time. Really see the landscape, the plants and creatures all around you. What can you hear? What can you smell? Is there water nearby? Sit quietly and take it all in.

Now imagine yourself changing, growing, becoming enormous, towering above everything. You're a tyrannosaurus rex, the king of your world. Nothing can harm you here. You could lie down and sleep in the open with nothing to fear.

This is an experience of pure fearlessness. Once you've had it, you can call it to mind whenever anxiety or panic starts to get to you, and it will help you breathe again!

⑧ So embarrassing!

One way of getting over something you feel embarrassed about is by making a funny story of it. Lots of successful comedians learnt how to do this in school as a sort of defence against bullying. Humour is a way of distancing yourself from strong emotions and making them safe.

Think of something embarrassing that happened to you. Imagine that you're watching it on TV and it's happening to one of your favourite soap or sitcom characters. Can you make it into a funny scene?

⑨ The old fear spring-clean

If you had no fear at all you'd probably be dead by now, squashed by a lorry or lost miles away from your parents' care and protection.

Some fears are just always useful, like fear of fire, but others you can grow out of. For example, if  you move to a new house you might feel nervous about getting lost when you go out, and that's a good fear because it will make you get directions or check a street map before you go out. But once you know your way around you can let go of it.

See if you can think of one thing that you needed to be afraid of once that you don't need to be afraid of any more.

⑩ I did it!

Think of something you were afraid of doing that you forced yourself to do. Fear is personal and it might be something other people wouldn't worry about at all. Write the story.

'I hadn't been in the burger bar since I dropped a bottle of coke on the floor there and it smashed everywhere and the manager got really angry and I felt so embarrassed I wanted the floor to swallow me up ...'

How did you feel after you had done it? 'Nobody recognised me and I wondered why I had made such a big deal of it and now I'll never worry about going in there again. Cashback!'

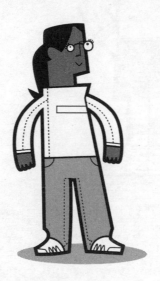

6 **SATURDAY**

Stand up for your rights

You have a right not to be bullied and if someone starts pushing you around you have a right to feel angry.

Your anger is like a huge hairy dog – very handy in a bullying situation ...

... but risky if you don't know how to control it.

It takes time and patience to train a dog and also to train your anger, but there's nothing complicated about it and, once you've done it, you've got a friend who will always be on your side.

Fight or flight ... or hang on a minute!

When anger kicks in, your first impulse is to fight or run away, and bullies and victims both tend to go with their first impulses. The slightest trigger can make a bully lash out or a victim crumble.

But both these knee-jerk reactions mean you miss out on the lovely positive power of anger. A fighter keeps fighting and a runner keeps running, completely at the mercy of their anger, when all the time they could be using it to help them get what they really want.

Are you at the mercy of your anger? Do the fight or flight quiz and find out.

Fight or flight – the anger quiz

A Your teacher keeps the whole class in at playtime for the fourth day in a row because one kid's being a pain. Do you

1   Go storming out.

2   Sit and seethe.

3   Complain to the head.

B Mum says it's your turn to wash up when it isn't. Do you

1   Shout and walk out.

2   Shut up and do it.

3   Explain that it's your brother's turn because you've done it three times in a row.

C Some little kid says your new haircut looks stupid. Do you

1   Give him a slap.

2   Collapse in tears.

3   Decide to ignore it.

D The boys are taking up the playground with football and you and your mates want to shoot some hoops. Do you

1   Grab the football off them and chuck it over the wall.

2   Mooch around feeling sorry for yourselves.

3   See if the lunchtime supervisor will help you work out a rota.

Results

Mostly 1 – Calm down! You've got the lovely energy of anger but instead of using it to get what you want you're letting it get you into trouble.

Mostly 2 – Your anger's got you on the run so fast you might not even have time to feel it.

Mostly 3 – You don't let anger press your buttons and that means no one else can either.

The secret of handling anger is not to react straight away. So when something makes you see red … stop, breathe, count!

Stop!

Even holding on for a few seconds can be long enough for you to feel the energy without running away, and to harness it so that it can't run away with you.

Breathe!

A single deep breath will help, but two or three are even better.

Count!

You might very well have seen your mum or dad do this when you left the living room in a complete mess or broke that hideous ornament they bought in Brighton before they got married.

There are several variations including

- counting slowly to ten under your breath.

- counting five objects you can see: '1 – teacup, 2 – sweater, 3 – magazine ...'

- describing five objects you can see: '1 – broken paving stone, 2 – greasy chip paper, 3 – smelly dog, 4 – shop with a sale on, 5 – blue bus.'

Stop-breathe-count gives you time to register that you feel angry, to control the fight-or-flight impulse and to start working out what you want to do about it.

What can you do?

Sometimes you can actually change the situation. For example, say someone's sending you abusive texts, you could get your phone company to block them. Result!

Sometimes you can argue your case. For example, say your mum won't let you get your ears pierced, you can tell her about all the other kids you know who've got pierced ears and say you'll pay for it from your savings and just generally plead. This won't always get the result you want, but it will mean you've stuck up for yourself by having your say. You have a right to be heard – but not necessarily a right to be right!

Sometimes you can't change the situation or have your say about it, and it feels like you can't do anything at all. But you can always do something – you can use your anger to defend yourself from feelings of self-doubt.

Tom and Lewis

Tom and Lewis went to after-school country dancing for a laugh but to their surprise, they both really enjoyed it, so they kept going. When the other boys in the class found out about it they teased them non-stop for being a pair of wusses.

Tom felt angry. He liked country dancing and he had a right to do what he liked. Was he going to let them spoil it for him? No! Why should he?

But Lewis felt anxious and upset. Maybe it was a bit wussy. Maybe he shouldn't enjoy it ... Instead of feeling angry with the other boys for being mean he ended up feeling fed up with himself for liking wussy stuff.

Bullying and teasing that's intended to hurt someone else is always wrong and it should make you angry. If it doesn't, you can end up like Lewis, turning it against yourself.

No!

What are the two most important letters in the alphabet?

N and O – you can't get on without them!

Angry feelings, if you listen to them, always say, 'No! This is not all right for me!' They ask you to check out what's going on and do something about it.

Even if the only thing you can do is to be absolutely clear in your own mind that there's nothing wrong with you and that you should be treated with respect, that's brilliant psychological self-defence. That's bully-busting!

So get rid of self-doubt and boost your self-belief by learning to handle your anger. Start now by dragging that big hairy anger-hound down to the bully-buster gym and choosing a Saturday training session.

Self-doubt

KiCK!

Choice of Saturday training sessions

❶ I get angry when ...

To spot your anger patterns, write this sentence out five times, filling in the gaps in a different way each time:

'I get angry when .... and then I ....'

For example, 'I get angry when Leanne calls me fat and then I want to cry/give her a slap/get a new best mate ...', 'I get angry when I get a bad grade and then I think I'm just stupid/screw my work up and throw it at someone/ make sure I do better next time ...'

❷ Stop, breathe, count!

Think of a time you were really angry with your mates. Did they shut you out or tease you or just annoy you by being stupid? Remember where you were – use your senses to bring it back more clearly – what can you see, hear, feel, smell and taste? Notice what's happening in your body as you spark up the old anger again. Anger can make you feel hot under the collar, skin prickling, pulse racing. Are you holding tension anywhere in your body?

Now stop. Hold it right there, still angry, but not lashing out or running away.

Breathe in slowly ... breathe out slowly ...

Count five objects you can see around you now –
'1, book – 2, curtain...'

What's happening in your body
now? Can you still feel the energy
of the anger?

Use the energy of the anger to
write the story (do a picture strip
if you don't like writing). Writing things down is
a great way of getting things out of your system.

❸ Put your anger in the frame

Find a picture in a magazine or on line that could
represent your anger. It might be a volcano, a
snarling tiger, a World War II fighter, a streak of
lightning ...

Stick it on a piece of paper that's big enough to
leave a margin all the way around.

Now decorate the margin with your favourite
doodles, numbers, colours, words – anything
that's special to you.

This shows that your anger is smaller than you. It's
powerful but you can contain it and not let it get
out of control.

❹ The anger line

Think of ten words that can mean angry – for example, furious, disappointed (that's your dad talking!), cross ...

Write them down on ten pieces of paper.

Place them in order on the floor, from the mildest to the strongest.

Walk the anger line, pausing at each word to feel the energy at the different stages.

❺ Your own bill of rights

Write a list of five things that make you angry, for example, 'Getting told off for something I didn't do.'

Reframe them as rights, for example, 'I have a right not to get told off for something I didn't do.'

Check whether you give these same rights to others.

⑥ The anger flip

Reread the story of Tom and Lewis (page 100–101), pausing after each sentence to really picture it.

Imagine that you're Tom. Can you feel his anger? Can you feel his power?

Now imagine that you're Lewis. How does it feel when you can't be angry with people who are nasty to you? Can you feel the flip as the anger rebounds on to yourself?

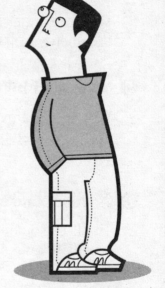

⑦ Take a deep breath

Do this sitting or standing up straight. Start with a few normal breaths, and then breathe in slowly, filling your lungs from the bottom up. Push your belly out first and then feel your whole chest expand right up to the top as you draw the air in.

Hold the breath for a count of three, and then slowly let the air out, starting from the top of your chest and finishing by pulling your stomach in.

Take a few normal breaths and then repeat it, noticing how your body is feeling.

This technique combines taking a deep breath with counting and it's a really effective way of calming your body, thoughts and emotions so that you don't have to lash out or fall apart the minute someone crosses you.

Note: You can use this technique any time you feel upset or agitated.

❽ A good cause

Think of something that makes you mad – say, cruelty to animals or not enough Simpsons on TV.

Write a list of things you could do to change the situation.

⑨ Be energised

Think of something that's annoyed you during the day – like being kept in at dinner-time, or having to stand up on the bus.

Feel the tension build as your body gets ready for fight-or-flight.

Use the energy to power you on a brisk walk or run or any other vigorous exercise.

⑩ Anger good – aggression bad

Feeling angry is a natural appropriate response to stuff like bullying – it makes me furious! Saying that you feel angry is OK as well. But it isn't OK to be aggressive when something annoys you.

Everyone gets it wrong sometimes, so think of a time you behaved aggressively by shouting, swearing, threatening, throwing things, shoving ...

How could you have handled it better? Is there any way you could have expressed your anger without treating anyone disrespectfully?

7 SUNDAY

Celebrate success!

I started the first chapter with my definition of bullying and I'm going to start the last one with my definition of success:

> Success is having the courage to try.

It doesn't make any difference whether you achieve your goal or not because so long as you keep it in sight and keep trying, every failure is a step along the way.

You can never just decide what you want and have it instantly – you have to work at it.

Supposing you want to be a great skateboarder, for example, you can't just jump on and be brilliant. You have to fall off lots of times to find out what doesn't work, and, once you've got the basic technique, you have to keep practising and pushing yourself to try new stuff if you want to get better. Trying new stuff means you're going to fall off lots of times ... and so it goes on.

Bully-busting takes time to master. It takes practice. You're bound to have struggles and setbacks but that doesn't matter – if you've read this far and done some training sessions then you've completed a whole successful week of bully-busting, and that calls for a celebration.

'But what's the point in celebrating?' I hear you say. 'Those knuckleheads are still treating me like something they've trodden in.'

Ahem, I think you've forgotten something. Bully-busting isn't about them ...

It's about you!

When you're feeling strong you can let teasing and name calling go like water off a duck's back, sticks and stones and all that.

When you're feeling strong, you can ask for help if you need it, supposing things get physical.

But if you get bogged down by victim feelings, you've got a problem because then you can't do anything to defend yourself at all.

Bullies want you to feel miserable and wimpy – if you feel happy and in control, they lose! So bully-busting is all about getting to feel OK and staying that way – that's the goal to keep in sight, and celebration is another great move towards it.

It's great to celebrate

Celebrating your successes is a way of nurturing yourself and that's particularly important when other people are being horrible to you. It also helps you to notice what you've achieved.

Your story

Imagine this is your story. All through school, you've been teased about your mum being fat – 'Is the hippo picking you up today?' they say, and 'You must be so puny because she eats all the food!' It makes you feel ashamed of your mum, and that makes you feel ashamed of yourself.

Outside school, they send you text messages, so you can never get away. You text back, pleading with them to stop, but they don't. You feel so miserable you just want to die.

After the first week of bully-busting, here I am asking you to celebrate, and there they are still sending you texts and I bet you feel like chucking the book at me, but wait ...

Celebrating means thinking about what you've achieved. On Monday you checked the websites and found out you should never answer abusive texts, so you stopped pleading. Sooo disappointing for the bullies! On Tuesday you wrote a letter telling them what you thought and sticking up for your mum – you didn't send it but, oh boy – it felt good! On Wednesday you did the secret message and noticed some great things about your life – including your lovely cuddly mum. On Thursday you watched a funny film and cracked a smile. On Friday you did 'So embarrassing' and saw the funny side of squeezing into your ma's little car beside her. On Saturday you got energised and used your anger to power your fastest-ever time at athletics club.

So they're still being mean, but that's just them. In your story, things are looking up, and you made that happen

So what are you waiting for? The streamers are up in the bully-buster gym and there are paper hats and sausages on sticks and lovely loud music all laid on just for you – go bully-buster!

Choice of Sunday celebrations

❶ The imaginary party

Imagine you're having a party to celebrate a whole successful week of bully-busting. Write a guest list of all the people you know who support you when you try new things and are pleased to see you do well. These may include your teacher, parents, grandparents, mates ...

It will be a very random bunch of people – that's why this party is imaginary!

❷ Your awesome A to Z

Write an A to Z of the first things that come into your head. This will be completely unique to you – if ten thousand people did it, no one would have the same things. Celebrate your uniqueness!

A is for antelope I've seen on TV.

B is for breakfast, which is usually toast.

C is for carbon dioxide – I don't know why I thought of that!

D is for disaster movies, which I don't generally like.

E is for the Easter bunny ...

❸ Share the pleasure

Celebration is about enjoying yourself, and you can enjoy yourself even more if you share the pleasure. So do one thing today just because it's nice – share your sweets, hold the door for your teacher, give your neighbour a cheery smile, email someone a funny joke ... you don't have to plan it. Just be on the lookout and an opportunity will arise.

❹ Brilliant bully-busting!

Lie down on your bed, close your eyes and take three deep breaths, nice and slow, to calm your mind.

Think about a bullying incident that has happened to you. Prepare yourself – you're going in!

Imagine the scene as if you already had brilliant bully-busting powers. You're mentally prepared – you know what you're going to do. If it gets physical you'll get help and if it doesn't, sticks and stones ... You feel good because you know that you're OK and they're the one with the problem. It's no way going to spoil your day.

OK, so you're nervous – who wouldn't be?

You can handle it. You're angry too, because they're out of order and you have a right not to be abused, but that just makes you more determined than ever not to let them get to you.

Now picture yourself walking away – cool, calm, happy, in control. They're picking their chins up off the floor. How good does it feel?

Really enjoy the moment and let that feeling inspire you to start another fabulous bully-busting week.

❺ Do something lovely

Organise a little treat, something you like doing but don't do every day. For example, curl up with the latest Jacqueline Wilson, go swimming, bowling or to the cinema, borrow a great new DVD, have a picnic or day trip, play some board games, visit a museum or gallery ...

If you're short of ideas, ask your family and friends what their idea of a little treat would be. They might surprise you!

❻ Champion's laurels

In ancient times, champions were given a crown of laurel leaves.

Fold a strip of paper over six times, concertina-fashion.

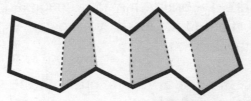

Draw a laurel leaf on it, going over the folded edges like this:

Cut round it, open the paper up and voila – your very own champion's laurels! Write a day of the week on each leaf and put which training session you did: 'Monday – manure ... Tuesday – Dear diary ...'

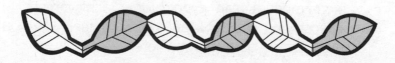

❼ Super-brilliant you

Take a virtual tour of your body and think about all the amazing things it can do.

Start at the top of your head. (Wow! Hair growing all the time – how incredible is that?) Work your way down – brain (thinking, imagining, sending instructions to the rest of your body) – eyes, ears, mouth ...

Notice the things that happen all the time, like breathing and blood pumping round, and the things you can do when you want to, like walk, run, write, eat and stroke the dog.

Your body is a super-brilliant aspect of super-brilliant you.

❽ Congratulations!

Write yourself a letter of congratulations on your week of bully-busting. Mention all the things you tried, not just the ones that went well.

Remember it's an even bigger achievement to keep trying and stick at it when it feels like you aren't really getting anywhere.

⑨ Happy to be me

Write a list of ten things that make you feel happy to be you. These will be your joys and pleasures, hopes and dreams and special people.

For example – 1, I live on a farm, 2, I'm going to be an architect, 3, Poggles (the best dog in the world), 4, OK big sis, 5, I'm good at drawing ...

⑩ Winner's fizz

Champagne is the traditional drink of winners but I think it's actually a bit disappointing. You can make a much more exciting winner's fizz like this:

1. Three-quarters fill a tall glass with anything fizzy.

2. Drop a dessert spoonful of ice cream into it for a foamy explosion – kerbam!

3. Sprinkle with toppits or choccy flakes.

4. Put your straw in.

5. Enjoy!

The Sunday bonus

Remember to buy yourself a little gift and wrap it up for a big celebration at the end if you're going for the full ten weeks.

Keep it up, bully-busters!

Being bullied can make even the most confident person feel like a victim, and once victim feelings have set in they can be hard to shake. That's why there are enough training sessions here for you to do a different one every day for ten weeks. By the end of that time, you'll be a black belt in bully-busting!

And finally ...

Two top top-up tips

1   If you love the art of bully-busting, there's no need to stop. It only takes a few minutes a day, it'll keep your self-esteem in tip top condition and it has absolutely no unwanted side effects.

2   If you find anything that works really well for you, make it part of your normal life. Lots of people throughout the world use things like mind messages, saying thank you and calming deep breaths every day. So can you!

it happens!

it makes
great manure!

By the same author

Bullies, Bigmouths and So-called Friends

'This brill book is full of tips on how to build up your confidence and look after yourself. We like!' Bubble

'At last a book that really helps you to deal with the people in your life who are making you miserable.' The Bookseller

'Unique in teaching children how to boost their self-esteem and so prevent bullying from affecting their lives.' The Independent

'Offers simple strategies for building up confidence so that taunts and teasing have fewer insecurities to feed on.' Sainsbury's Magazine

'There is much in this book that children might find of real help.' Books for Keeps

'An ideal book to be used in schools.' ChildLine in Schools

'The ideal book for teachers and counsellors ... as well as children themselves.' Education Today

Visit the author's website
www.jennyalexander.co.uk